Dog Training:

20 Smart Dog Tricks You Can Teach Your Dog

SHANNON O'BOURNE

"Dog Training" by Shannon O'Bourne. Published by Walnut Publishing
Company, Hanover Park, IL 60133

www.walnutpub.com

BONUS: BOOK CLUB INVITE

Before we get started with this Dog Training book, we wanted to tell you how much we appreciate you as a reader, and that we want to invite you to our Free Book Club.

When you subscribe, you get first access to discounted and free new releases from our small publishing house, Walnut Publishing.

Claim your invite at www.walnutpub.com.

Thanks for buying, and enjoy reading.

NOTE FROM THE AUTHOR

Thank you for purchasing "Dog Training: 20 Smart Dog Tricks You Can Teach Your Dog."

I hope you will learn a lot of valuable information that you can apply to your own life, as well as have some fun and be entertained!

I worked hard to write this book with you, my reader, in mind. Whether you enjoyed the book, or you think I got some things wrong, I'd love to hear from you.

I personally read all my reviews on Amazon, and love to hear from my readers. If you can take a minute to just write at least one line about what you thought of my book, I'd be really grateful.

Type this URL into your browser to go straight to the review page for this book: bit.ly/dogtricksreview

I really appreciate it, and now, let's get to the book!

—Shannon O'Bourne

TABLE OF CONTENTS

1 INTRODUCTION

THANK YOU FOR BUYING THIS dog training guide! I'm so glad you're taking the first step toward a better-behaved dog, a better relationship with your furry best friend, and that you're ready to try out a bunch of fun tricks to challenge you and your dog.

I hope to guide you on your way toward becoming the type of dog owner who your dog looks up to, admires, respects and trusts.

Dog training — and teaching dog tricks — is all about building a solid foundation of communication and respect between you and your dog.

In this book, you'll learn everything you need to know about dog training in the first few chapters before diving in to teaching your dog the 5 essential basic commands and 15 more amazing tricks. We'll go over dog behavior, clicker training, and the right training method to use for the tricks.

I hope both you and your dog will learn something new, and have fun in the process! Let's get started!

2 THE WELL-BEHAVED DOG

IN THIS FIRST CHAPTER, WE will look at what it means to have a well-behaved dog, as a dog that listens to you is a prerequisite to teaching any fun tricks!

We all want our dog to be the best behaved dog on the block. Having a disrespectful, rambunctious and uncontrollable dog leads to problems not just for you as an owner, but problems for your dog as well. Your dog may not understand how to interact with people, other dogs, or the world around him or her. This can be not only annoying and frustrating on a repeated day-to-day basis, but dangerous if an accident were to happen.

So what's the solution to the poorly behaved dog? Dog training.

Dog Training is the Key to a Healthy Dog

Believe it or not, some owners just don't believe in dog training. They rely on the natural instincts of the dog, failing to correct behavior properly or teach their dog how to navigate the world. But you are your dog's shepherd. As his or her owner, you are responsible for your dog, and you are your dog's teacher, partner, master, best friend and ally. If you fail to show your dog the proper way to behave, he or she will feel reckless, abandoned, and confused.

Like young children exploring their boundaries, dogs want to know what is expected of them. They crave normalcy, routine and understandable consequences. A dog understands that they get fed at a certain time each morning. They understand that their dog bed is where they can sleep, and not your mattress. Without this knowledge, dogs feel out of routine, unsure of themselves, and constantly unsure of what boundaries exist and what behavior is expected of them.

Patience is Key

At first when training your dog, they will be testing boundaries to see what is appropriate. This is the way your dog learns, and you should remember to go slow, be patient and try to understand why your dog is acting the way he or she is.

A dog is an animal, and they cannot reason the way that we humans do. But with proper training, as outlined in this book, your dog can come to learn just what is expected of them, and you can have a well-behaved dog with great manners. You can have a dog that respects people, other dogs, and most importantly, you. Then your relationship can flourish in a healthy environment.

Your dog has an incredibly well-behaved dog hiding inside him or her, and it is up to you to bring it out of them!

Work with Your Dog's Natural Instincts

When training your dog, it will be important to remember their animal instincts. That is why we will use treats as rewards, as almost nothing is more satisfying to a dog than an extra-special treat.

We will also be working within your dog's natural drives, and not against them. Dogs are descended from wolves, and they like being a part of the pack, having order, and understanding their place in the pack. By training your dog, you will be teaching your dog this important role.

This does not mean extreme dominance, or showing your power over your dog, as some trainers will have you believe. It just means that working together is most important for your dog, as well as developing a relationship with you based on expectations and understanding.

Get Ready for Training

So what can you expect to learn from this book?

In the following chapters, we will discuss all the important basics your need to know to teach your dog commands, and then you will learn how to train 20 awesome tricks. We first include five basic commands, such as sit, down, stay, come and heel, as these commands are essential for moving on to more advanced tricks.

In the next chapter, you will learn about dog training myths. This book will only be using a positive reinforcement method. Dog training is most effective when it appeals to your dog's reward centers. If you use physical corrections, or negative reinforcement (punishing your dog instead of rewarding them), you will have a fearful, timid dog that does not understand why he or she is being attacked by you.

Then, in the next chapter, we will discuss the proper training environment you need for your dog. Environment is a key to success. If you do not have the proper calm environment, you will be setting up your dog for failure. You want to give your dog every chance to succeed.

Then we will do a brief overview of an introduction to clicker training. Clicker training is the most accurate and effective method of training, and clickers can be purchased extremely cheaply, so it makes sense to purchase this essential training tool. You will learn how and why to use the training clicker.

The last chapter before we get to the tricks will be about the right training method. You will learn the essential steps, tips and tricks that are needed to train your dog a new behavior, and these are the things that will be essential across all the different commands.

The Five Essential Tricks for Any Dog

In the chapters after the ones about dog training methods, you can expect to learn the essential tricks you need to teach your dog if you want him or her to have the very basics of good behavior down. Even if you don't want to teach your dog the fun tricks like roll over, holding food on their nose, shake, or other party tricks, your dog will at the very least need these five behaviors.

These five behaviors were selected because they help to contain your dog's movements. The five essential behaviors are sit, come, stay, down and heel.

These movements will be essential because your dog will face many instances over the course of his or her life where your dog needs to comply with expectations of a certain, specific situation. For example, during grooming, your dog needs to stay still and calm. It is the same for physical exams. At the dog park, you need to make sure your dog is well-behaved, or when you are hosting company at your home.

Did you know that all the behaviors that zookeepers "train" the animals in their care to do are functional? All the behaviors that a tiger, elephant or zebra are trained to perform are for medical checkups, health assessments, and the health and safety for both animal and zookeeper. So you can take a similar approach to the philosophy of training your dog: It is for the health and safety of both of you!

Sit is essential because this gets your dog to stay in one place. Come allows you to call your dog to you, in case they ever get off-leash or into a bad situation. Stay is a good way to start addressing separation anxiety, and making sure that your dog can control him or herself even if you are not near him or her. Down is essential because it can diffuse stressful situations with your dog. Heel is essential for walking your dog on a leash, an activity that every dog loves.

Training is About You and Your Dog

Overall, the purpose of training isn't to control your dog, but to make them live a happy, healthy life with you. It's like any relationship, whether animal or human: When everyone knows the boundaries, what is expected of them, and how to act around each other, everyone wins.

The process will be slow, but what you are building with your dog is important, essential, wonderful, and amazing, if you give it time to flourish. You will be communicating with your dog in a special language that you both understand, and that is truly an amazing phenomenon. You will basically be talking to your dog, and your dog will be talking back!

So spend time with your dog growing your relationship, and most importantly, having fun! Dog training can be a lot of fun with your pet, so get ready to learn all about dog training in this book.

Key Takeaways from This Chapter

- A well-trained dog understands his place in the world and his boundaries, making for a happier dog

- A well-trained dog is easier to live with for you, the owner

- Good dog training is relationship-based and focused on trust, communication and mutual expectations and understanding

- The five essential commands every dog should know are sit, down, stay, come and heel

- In this book, you will be learning to "talk" to your dog, and have your dog "talk" back!

3 Dog Training Myths

As with any type of interaction with animals, there exists a spectrum of philosophies, and it seems everyone has an opinion. Some people think it is OK to physically punish animals; others fight for animal rights. No matter where you fall on the spectrum of your philosophy of the way animals and humans should interact, share the world, and treat each other, you have picked up this dog training book to improve your dog's behavior.

We have our own philosophy of dog training, which is entirely based on positive reinforcement, and strengthening the relationship between you and your dog and building it, not destroying it with harshness, physical punishment, or negative reinforcement of any kind.

In this chapter, we'll talk a bit more about our philosophy of positive, relationship-based dog training, and why any type of negative-based dog training is not effective. Here are some dog training myths:

Myth #1: Negative reinforcement is a strong training tool

The first myth we will discuss is explaining what the general concept of negative reinforcement is.

Negative reinforcement is removing a stimulus that your dog does not like. For example, if you are training your dog to not jump on the couch, if you shout at him while he is on the couch, he dislikes this loud, angry yelling. When he performs the behavior you want, which is to jump down from the couch, you stop yelling, therefore removing the action that he dislikes. You are reinforcing his good behavior in this way.

Positive punishment is adding a stimulus that your dog does not like following a bad behavior. For example, if you do not want your dog to bark as much, you may use a shock collar to shock him each time he barks. He is being punished with a stimulus that he doesn't like every time he does the wrong behavior.

So what is positive reinforcement, the training philosophy we will be using?

Positive reinforcement is presenting your dog with a stimulus he likes after doing a good behavior.

For example, if we take the last two examples, you can see how those would be dealt with through positive reinforcement.

In the first example, training your dog to not jump on the couch can be achieved by rewarding the dog for understanding the command "off." For barking, you can train your dog to understand the command "quiet" by using positive reinforcement.

In positive reinforcement, the dog is rewarded for good behavior, thereby reinforcing those wanted behaviors. The dog associates something it desires, like pets, cuddles, food, praise, toys, play time, a walk, or anything positive, with the good action.

In the next section, we'll talk about common dog training methods that fall under the "punishment" category, and therefore, are not recommended by this book.

Myth #2: Shock or Training Collars Work Well

There are many myths surrounding dog training, and as we discussed, we will not advocate anything that physically, mentally or emotionally is meant to punish a dog.

What are these instruments? A shock collar is a dog collar that can administer a small shock to your dog on command through a remote control. They can also be referred to as zap collars, electronic collars, e-collars, and remote training collars. They are most often used on the neck but can be placed anywhere on the dog's body.

A training collar is usually a "choke" collar or "prong" collar. These collars are made out of chains, and some have spikes on the inside of the collar to rest against the dog's throat, while others are just chains with no spikes. In both forms, the point of the collar is to effectively "choke" the dog, presenting such a negative sensation that the dog is dissuaded from the behavior it is doing.

If you put your hands around your own neck, you will feel how sensitive this area of your body is. Would you like to have prongs or chains squeezing you here? A dog's throat is similar in construction, and also sensitive.

Even if people argue that shock or training collars have such a small impact on your dog that they are not actually physically painful, the shock and training collars are still harmful in that they harm your relationship with your dog, and nothing will be more harmful to your dog than breaking down this relationship as his friend, teacher, guide, protector, and best friend.

Punishment can often be seen as a "quick fix" for dog training and behavior by people. It can be very effective in the short term, as if your dog feels both physical and emotional pain, feeling scared, anxious, weak and intimidated by you, it is less likely to do the behavior that it was punished for.

But in the long term, your dog will develop other behavioral issues due to being treated in a punishing way, behaviors that are much more deep-seated and difficult to address.

Therefore, we never recommend the use of shock or training collars in dog training.

Myth #3: Dogs Need to Be Dominated

There is a common training myth that because dogs are descended from wolves and are pack animals, they need to understand that you are the "Alpha" of the pack and dominate and control them.

This is not true. Dogs are far from the hierarchy of their wild ancestors. Dogs are called "man's best friend" for a reason, not "man's best intimidated subject."

Training your dog is forming a partnership, one that should not be based on exerting power, control, domination, or any other intense, hierarchy-based philosophies.

Of course, you are a human, and you do have a lot more control over your dog. But exerting this power over your dog only makes them nervous, fearful, and reactive.

A good training relationships should be based on mutual respect. Respect you dog's autonomy, ability to learn, and effort he puts toward his training. He may make mistakes, or not be perfect, but neither will you! Communicating with a dog is tough, just like communicating with a human can be tough for a dog. That is OK. You will work together and grow your relationship despite your challenges.

Working together as a team is always a better position to come from than feeling superior and dominant over your dog in your training.

Myth #4 Some Dogs are Just Bad Dogs

This is another common myth that people have about dog training. They can believe that their dog is just too distracted, hyper, dumb, or otherwise just a "bad dog" and cannot learn.

This is not the case, and a harmful mindset to have. Just like people, dogs learn in all different ways and at all different speeds. It is important to remember that your training will need to be tailored to your dog, and it is in your best interest and your dog's to be patient, forgiving, and understanding when your dog is having trouble with a concept or grasping a behavior.

With enough patience, love, and by following the techniques that we recommend, a dog is always able to become a good dog. Sometimes, professional training help is needed. But even if you need to hire a trainer, trying to train your dog yourself will have many benefits.

Follow Your Gut

Building a relationship with your dog is important no matter what, and even if you feel you don't succeed in training your dog commands an tricks, working with him or her on a daily basis, giving treats, and practicing communication will go a long way toward both of your happiness in the long run.

Overall, you should only do what you feel comfortable doing with your dog. If you go to a pet store, a group training class, or just talk to people at the dog park, they may recommend negative reinforcement or punishment for your dog. Be polite, but in the end, stick with only what you are comfortable with for your dog.

Your relationship to your dog matters above all, and earning your dog's trust is important.

In the next chapter, we'll discuss the right training environment to give your dog the best chance of success in learning the five essential commands that every dog should know.

Key Takeaways from This Chapter

- Positive reinforcement is the best training method

- Negative reinforcement and positive punishment should be avoided as training methods

- Shock collars and training (or choke) collars can hurt your dog, and they can damage your relationship even more

- There are no "bad dogs," just untrained dogs

- Trust your gut when training and don't do anything that makes you uncomfortable

4 THE RIGHT TRAINING ENVIRONMENT

HAVING THE RIGHT TRAINING ENVIRONMENT for your dog is essential, and could be the difference between success and failure in teaching the commands in this book.

Let's find out what the best training environment consists of.

Avoid as Many Distractions as Possible

Imagine you were trying to learn, perhaps in a math class, history class, or English literature class. You did your best to pay attention to the teacher, but instead of taking place in a classroom, the location of your desk and the blackboard was in the middle of an amusement park.

There were the sounds of people screaming on roller coasters as they roared above your head, the pings and lights of the carnival games section that you could see just in the distance, and the smells of people walking by eating delicious hot dogs, churros, burgers, popcorn, ice cream and funnel cakes. People were having conversations around you, or calling out to each other. Kids were running about.

It wouldn't be as easy to memorize historical dates, understand old English, or grasp a Calculus concept in this learning environment, would it?

It's the same for your dog. Dogs experience the world differently than humans do. Even if you try to train your dog in your backyard, where you think there are not too many distractions, there could be many for your dog.

There are squirrels, rabbits, bugs, the sounds of airplanes, cars, perhaps children in neighbors' yards. There may be people cutting their grass a few houses down, a cookout happening on the next block, or the air may be forecasting a rain soon to come.

All of these sights, smells, sounds and experiences are intense for dogs, more so than the less sensitive senses of humans. It could feel like being in the middle of that crazy amusement park to your dog.

So you want to give your dog every opportunity to succeed, and make it as easy as possible for him or her to learn, listen, and pay attention to the most important thing: you!

In the next section, we'll discuss what makes a good classroom for your dog.

Familiar, Indoor and Quiet is Best

A dog is best trained in a calm, quiet, familiar environment with as few distractions as possible.

The best place to start is a room inside your home that your dog is familiar with. There won't be fun new smells to explore, items to look at, or anything unfamiliar.

At the same time, even things that are familiar can be a distraction for a dog. If a favorite toy is present, or other people are home and constantly walking in and out of the room, even though the dog is used to these things, they are still stimulating. Remove the possibility of any distraction. If you live with other people, let them know you will be doing training with the dog and they should avoid the room you are in for 30 minutes or however long you will train. Let them know not to make loud noises or cook delicious food in the next room over, either.

Remove all favorite toys or items your dog finds especially distracting.

Turn off the TV and radio and anything making sound. Allow your dog the chance to give you his full attention. In the next section, we'll talk about your dog's approach to training.

A Good Environment Includes a Dog in a Good Mood

Even if all the environmental factors are aligned and you have a calm, quiet, familiar and distraction-free space, your dog still needs to come to the training in the right mood.

That means timing is also important.

You shouldn't do a training session with your dog right before a meal time, or right after a vet appointment. It shouldn't be when your dog is resting after a long day of walks, playing and running. He should be alert, have energy, and not have recently done something out of the ordinary like get groomed.

Pay attention to how your dog seems. Does he seem very hyper, distracted, or sleepy? These may not be good times to train.

As your dog becomes more advanced in training, these things won't matter as much. But in the beginning, you need to give your dog as many chances to succeed as possible. He will need to get used to training, so introducing it slowly is best, and trying to make it as routine as possible.

For example, if you do dog training every day at 10 a.m. for 12 minutes, your dog will come to expect this routine and look forward to training. He will be excited to perform well for you and receive treats and praise.

Keeping your dog in an attentive, alert and good mood also means taking frequent breaks from training. Training can be mentally strenuous for a dog. They have much shorter attention spans than we humans do. Doing an intense repetition of a command for three minutes, and then taking three minutes off for pets is a good variance.

If you are just drilling your dog with commands for 20 minutes straight, he will become bored, frustrated and his energy will be drained.

The Best Treats for Training

The best way to use positive reinforcement to train your dog for good behavior is to use food treats as rewards.

While praise and petting are also rewarding, they are not as strong of reinforcements, so it is best to stick with a consistent use of food in the beginning with training your dog. You can add praise and petting in addition, but make sure your dog gets food each time he does something right.

Healthy treats are best, as you don't want training to mean that your dog packs on the pounds! The food should not be kibble that your dog eats for meals, as this is not special.

Treats should also be small, as you will be repeating training commands often, so your dog will be getting many small treats at once, every day. Some good, safe treats for dogs are pieces of carrot, apple, green beans, or chicken. There are also ready-made training treats you can buy online or at local pet food stores.

Be careful with what "human foods" you feed to your dog, however. Do not feed your dog onions, grapes, raisins, chocolate or avocado, as these foods are harmful to a dog's system and can even cause death. Always Google something before you feed it to your dog, just to be safe!

In the next chapter, you will get an introduction to another item we will be using to train your dog, in addition to treats: the clicker.

Key Takeaways from This Chapter

- Dogs face many more distractions in sound, smell and sight than humans

- Choose an indoor space that is quiet, familiar, calm and distraction-free for your dog's training sessions

- Train your dog when he is alert, attentive and not hyper, sleepy, or a meal time is approaching

- Train your dog with small, healthy treats and always Google a "human food" before feeding to check that it isn't dangerous to dogs

5 INTRODUCTION TO CLICKER TRAINING

CLICKER TRAINING IS A TYPE of training that uses positive reinforcement. Clickers can be quite easy to find, and you can pick them up for usually less than $2 at a local pet supply store, or get a package of several delivered from a shop online in case you lose one.

In this chapter, we will give you an overview of the philosophy of clicker training so you understand why it is important to use one. We will also discuss how clicker training works and how you will use it with your dog to achieve success in learning the basic commands and more.

Learning How to Learn

Teaching your dog clicker training means teaching your dog how to learn. Beginning a training regimen with a dog means activating new parts of the dog's brain, just like if you were to take up piano with no musical experience, or start learning a foreign language.

In fact, learning how to communicate with a human is like learning a foreign language for a dog. Just like how *you* are learning the foreign language of how to communicate with your dog, too! You will both be speaking a new, simple language based in body language, trust, a few words, and predictable actions and responses.

What is a Clicker, and How Will We Use It?

A clicker is a small, plastic device, usually on a key chain. It has a button you press, or a piece of metal, that makes a loud "CLICK" sound.

The click will be what you use to signal to your dog that they have completed a command correctly.

The click needs to be, above all else, precise in its timing in two ways. The first way the click needs to be precise is that it must happen immediately at the end of the desired behavior from your dog. It cannot happen too long after, but right as your dog's bottom hits the floor, for example when you are teaching sit. You must click just at that moment, so your dog associates his sit with the click.

A click means that the desired behavior has ended. If you are doing a sit and stay command with your dog, you do not click after sit, but after stay. If you click after sit but do not give food, this is confusing for your dog. A click should always, always mean a reward. A click should only happen at the end of the behavior you want to see from your dog and are training for.

The click must be precise in another manner of timing. The click must be precise in that it happens before and separately from giving the food reward. The click needs to be important to your dog. It means that a reward will come, so once your dog understands that a click means he will be receive food within a few seconds, the click will become as satisfying and rewarding as actually receiving the food.

But for your dog to associate the click with food properly, the dog must be 100% focused on the click. For the dog to be focused on the click, that means he cannot be distracted by anything else that could signal food. You should not be reaching for your pocket, looking towards where you have food, or doing anything other than giving a click sound and remaining still. Dogs are very sensitive to slight eye movements and body movements, and will pick up on the smallest change in your body language. Only after you have clicked can you reach for the food and give it to your dog.

What is most important here is to understand that the click is not simultaneous with food, but food is given immediately, as soon as possible, after the click.

This may seem difficult, but it just takes practice to get it right. Once you have the rhythm down, and you and your dog are both used to that rhythm, it will be second-nature and you won't even think about it.

In the beginning though, you will need to practice. But there is a great opportunity to practice, and that is introducing your dog to the clicker.

Introducing Your Dog to Clicker Training

Introducing your dog to the clicker is the best way for you to practice your timing, and your dog to learn what the clicker means: food!

To introduce your dog to the clicker, you will be clicking and rewarding without asking for any behavior.

Make these sessions short but frequent in the days before you will start training your dog. The purpose is only to teach your dog to associate the sound of the click with the reward of the food.

Practice your timing in making the click separate from reaching for food. Do it when your dog is in different situations, but not when he is too distracted. For this exercise, you do not need to be as strict about your training environment, since all you are doing is having the dog learn that click means food. Repeat frequently throughout the day.

Importance of Clicker Training

Overall, clicker training is important because the more precise you are with your clicks, the more precise you can be with training your dog.

A click tells the dog that the behavior has been performed sufficiently. So if you click when your dog has his bottom a few inches off the ground, but not totally on the floor for the "sit" position, he has learned that it is enough to make the motion to sit, but he does not actually need to sit.

Dogs are very sensitive to stimuli, and if you can clicker train your dog well, you will have a more precise language with him.

Clicking will be your primary method of communicating with your dog on this training journey, and the better you communicate, the stronger your relationship with your dog will be, and the more successful your training sessions.

In the next chapter, the last before we get to the basic command how-to's, we will go over the last basic things you need to know to be the most effective dog trainer you possibly can.

Key Takeaways from This Chapter

- Clicker training means teaching your dog how to learn

- A clicker is a small plastic device that makes a CLICK sound when pressed

- Your dog will learn that one click equals one reward

- Clicks need to be precise in timing in two ways: A click should happen at the end of a behavior, and separately but immediately before food is given

- The more precise your clicker training, the more precise your communication with your dog

6 THE RIGHT TRAINING METHOD

IN THE FIRST FOUR CHAPTERS of this book, you learned a lot about why training your dog is important, the philosophy behind training your dog with positive reinforcement, choosing the right environment, and how to use clicker training.

In this last chapter, you will learn some final steps you need to know before diving in to teaching your dog his first command! Read these final tips to get prepared to spend some quality time with your dog.

What is a Trick?

Let's break it down: What is a trick, a behavior, or a command that you teach your dog? Each of these words is interchangeable, at least in our use.

A trick is a series of movements that your dog does to complete an overarching behavior goal you have in mind, which is rewarded with the click.

However, sometimes your dog may need more step-by-step instructions. For instance, for a sitting trick, you might think the trick cannot get any more basic than "sit." But it still can be broken down. It starts with your dog facing you. Your dog should also be standing. Then the dog lowers his back half. It is lowered all the way to the ground. His bottom is on the ground for at least a second. This is a sit in several steps.

Some tricks your dog may get right away, while other tricks may need to be broken down into pieces. This is where you may need to get creative. You need to really think about what the most basic movements are of a behavior, and how you can click-reward them. We will have some ideas for you in the trick chapters of this book.

Next, let's look at how you will begin each trick in the commands section of this book during your training sessions.

The Beginning of Every Trick

To begin each training session, you will need a pocket full of healthy treats that are dog-safe and small. You will need your clicker. You will need a quiet, distraction-free space.

You will need yourself and your dog (of course!) Choose a good time that is not right before a meal time or walk, not when your dog is neither bursting with energy nor very sleepy.

Bring your dog into the training room with you, and since you have already trained for click = food (if not, go back to Chapter 4: Introduction to Clicker Training and learn how to do this introduction), your dog can be introduced to the training session with a click and food reward.

The first thing you need from your dog for a successful training session is to get their attention. They have already associated a click with food, so now they should associate giving you attention with food.

If your dog is well-mannered to begin with, standing in front of you calmly while waiting for your instruction may be natural. If your dog is a little more rambunctious, you may need to clicker-train to get him or her calmly standing in front of you before moving on to learning sit, down, stay, come, and heel.

If you need to train for "calm," for example, use the command calm, and do not click until your dog has settled a bit.

Training: Rapid but Calm

Remember when you are training that you will need to take frequent breaks, especially at first. Give your dog (and yourself!) a mental and behavioral rest to do whatever you like. Give some pets or belly rubs, or let your dog have a run in the yard. Sessions shouldn't be longer than 10-20 minutes at first, and they should have breaks at least every few minutes.

When you are training, clicks and commands should be rapid. Rapid training is the best way to get your dog to understand a repeated behavior. So train quickly, but take frequent breaks.

Sometimes dogs may seem unfocused or bored with training if they are not performing well, but it may be because they don't understand that they are meant to be getting treats. If you click every few seconds, the rapid treats should be enough to get your dog re-interested in the training.

In addition to your dog being calm, you should also be calm. Your body language, voice tone and level, and behavior should be relaxed, authoritative, and self-assured. If you are excited, loud or move your body too much, it will be distracting for your dog, and there will be so many other behaviors that your dog may associate with clicks and rewards than the ones you are going for. Isolate the single behavior as much as possible.

Make your dog do the work in the training. Have your dog come to you to get treats, and don't encourage or give your dog "hints" too often on the right behavior, otherwise they will come to rely on these hints, and not really learn the trick and associate it all by themselves.

You are the Best Person to Train Your Dog

At this point in the book, you may feel a bit overwhelmed, and that is totally normal. We have covered a lot of material, and your head is probably swirling with "to-do's" and "not-to-do's," and you are nervous you will not be a good enough dog trainer.

Like anything in life, starting a new skill is intimidating, difficult and scary. We want to be great, but it is nearly impossible to be great at anything you are trying for the first time.

Be patient with yourself and your dog as you both start to learn this new dimension of your relationship. If you follow the guides and tips in this book to the best of your ability, you will do great! You won't "mess up" your dog, as long as you stay away from punishment or negative reinforcement and only use the positive reinforcement method outlined.

Just do your best, and you will start to see improvements in your confidence, training ability, and communication with your other half, your dog.

Don't get discouraged at the start if things aren't going well. Building a habit is putting in the work a little over many days. You are not looking for instant results, but building the foundation of your relationship with your dog brick-by-brick (and trick-by-trick) as his teacher, guide, companion, and best friend.

You are the best person to train your dog. You and your dog share a home and a life together, and you are bonded in a way no one else is. Be confident, and your dog will feed off your confidence and be confident as well. Remember, dogs are very sensitive to human behavior and emotions, and your dog will be able to tell what you are feeling. Help your dog by being a great role model for your training sessions, and you will find your dog feeling more comfortable, confident and proud, if you do, too.

One last note: Have fun! Whether or not you are successful in training your dog, you are working on your relationship and doing a fun activity together, and that is what counts: quality time with your beloved dog.

Alright, new trainers, it's time to release you to the essential tricks section of this book, in which you will learn how to teach your dog to sit, down, stay, come and heel.

Good luck to you and your dog!

Key Takeaways from This Chapter

- A trick, command or behavior is a sequence of movements. Break a trick down into its smallest movement blocks if you are having trouble

- Come to each training session with treats, your clicker, a calm environment, a calm body and a calm dog

- Keep training sessions short and take frequent breaks

- Patience goes a long way, especially in the beginning

- You are the best person to train your dog, as you have a special bond no one else does

- Feel confident and relaxed going into your training and your dog will pick up on this and mirror you

- Have fun!

7 Introduction to 20 Dog Tricks

In this second section of this dog training book, we will get to the fun stuff: 20 fun and exciting dog tricks! The first five tricks are the essential commands:

- Sit
- Down
- Stay
- Come
- Heel

Then we'll learn 15 super fun tricks:

- Kiss (Licks)
- Bark on Command (Speak)
- Shake/High Five
- Fetch
- Go to Bed
- Roll Over
- Play Dead (Bang Bang!)
- Spin
- Sit Pretty (on Hind Legs)
- Leave It
- Yawn
- Bow

- Balance Item on Nose
- Get Leash
- Quiet (Stop Barking)

Alright, it's time to dive in!

8 SIT

TEACHING YOUR DOG HOW TO sit is an essential command. In fact, it's the first one we recommend teaching. When your dog is sitting, they can focus on you and learn follow-up commands like down, or more exciting tricks, like balancing an item on the nose.

As always, have a good training environment for your dog that is free of distraction and helps your dog be in a good mood for learning. You will need to have your healthy treats and your clicker ready for a training session. Also, be aware of your own body language and appear calm.

The first step is to get your dog's attention and click when he pays attention to you. This is the first step to show that a training session will begin. Then take out another treat, so he knows you have it. Place it over your dog's nose, and then slide it backwards over his snout and head. He will naturally try to follow the treat with his eyes and this will cause his backend to sit on the ground. As soon as his bottom touches the floor, say 'sit' and click and give a treat reward.

You can then release him from the command by stepping back and having him come to you so he is standing again. You can say 'free' or something if you like. If he doesn't move, take out another treat from your pocket, and this will definitely motivate him to move. Repeat this step, with moving the treat over the head, as many times as you like. Remember to break up training session and keep them short so as to not wear out your dog (or your patience!)

The next step is to stop moving the treat over your dog's head, but to just say the command 'sit.' Once your dog has mastered sit, you can move the training session to more distracting training locations to really reinforce the behavior.

Now, a few tips. If you find that your dog is energetic during training, you can start training sessions by keeping him on a leash. Remember as well not to overuse the command 'sit' if your dog is not getting it at first, as this will make the phrase meaningless. He really needs to connect it to the act of sitting. And if your dog turns or walks instead of sitting naturally when you move the treat over his head, train in a corner of a room so he cannot walk around.

That is how to train the command 'sit.' Remember to heap lots of praise on your dog, as this is the first command you will use to start building up your training relationship.

9 DOWN

THE DOWN COMMAND MEANS GETTING your dog to lay down on command, and it follows naturally from the mastery of the sit command. As with all training sessions, choose a good environment and make sure your dog is in a good mood to train.

The first step is to have your dog sit, which you should already have mastered in the last chapter. Squat in front of your dog so you are facing him at eye-level. Move the treat from his nose downward so that he follows it with his head. Keep moving the treat until he follows it into the lying position. As he reaches the floor (partway or fully, whichever he naturally does first) say the 'down' command, click and reward. You may need to teach this trick in stages, with your dog going lower and lower, or he may pick up on the first try that he is supposed to lay his body all the way down on the ground.

Repeat these steps as many times as you need, and then as with the sit command, you can move on to training in more challenging environments. Remember to stop each training session before your dog loses interest, as you want him to leave feeling good about training, and not that it is something he wants to avoid in the future. Also remember to use spoken praise (like 'good dog!') and pets to reward your dog as well as the treats, so he enjoys the training session more.

10 STAY

NOW WE WILL LEARN THE 'stay' command, which also naturally comes after learning the 'sit' and 'down' commands of the last two chapters.

For this training session, you will first need to have your dog sit, and then have him lie down. Reward with treats for these behaviors. Never skip rewarding with treats. Now, take out a treat and command your dog to 'stay' while putting your hand out in front of you. If your dog doesn't move, then click and reward with a treat. Start the trick over with the sit and down commands. Command 'stay' again while staying in place, but then take one step backward and say the command again. If your dog stayed still, click and reward with the treat and praise. If your dog got up and came over to you, do not reward, as then he will associate coming to you with getting the reward. So withhold the reward in this case. Repeat the steps, and if your dog cannot stay in one place as your step backward, then just keep reinforcing 'stay' as he stays in one place and slowly work up to moving away from him.

As your dog begins to master staying in one place, add more and more steps to the stay command, even moving out of sight of your dog if he really gets good at the command. 'Stay' may be more difficult for your dog than the sit or down commands, as those commands were actions, but the 'stay' command involves doing nothing at all. Be patient and keep working on it over days or weeks. Some dogs will catch on faster than others. Another way to increase the difficulty of this trick is to add something distracting to the environment, like another person, or changing up the environment altogether.

11 Come

THE NEXT BASIC COMMAND WE will go over is the 'come' command, which gets your dog to come to you when called. It is a good idea to teach your dog the stay command first, as 'come' will be his natural instinct, and it may be harder to teach 'stay' after learning 'come.'

So for come, use the same training environment, same healthy treats, and make sure to prepare your own frame of mind before the training session. For this trick, you will need a leash, so make sure to have one on hand.

The first step is to have your dog leashed, standing about six feet away. Your dog can either be standing, or you can have them sit. Walk backward from your dog quickly, and use the 'come' command. The quick motion should entice them to follow (and make sure the leash is therefore longer than six feet). If your dog doesn't automatically follow, tug the leash a little bit to urge them forward (but do not pull). Reward whenever your dog follows you, and repeat the steps as many times as you like, but remembering to keep your training sessions short.

Increase the difficulty of learning this trick by removing the leash from your dog. It can be combined with the 'stay' command to practice that one as well. Use, 'stay,' wait for a bit, and then 'come,' and see if your dog understands.

12 HEEL

'HEEL' IS THE COMMAND THAT you will use when walking your dog to keep them from getting distracted, pulling on the leash, or generally being a bit rambunctious when on a walk. 'Heel' will tell your dog to stay at your side, walking at your pace. Of course, on walks it is good to let your dog do "dog things" and sniff around, explore the environment, and meet other dogs (if the other owner agrees). But being able to control your dog and tell them how to walk in some instances is important for their safety. If they get off-leash, or run towards a strange dog that could be dangerous, you want to be able to call them back.

Going for a walk is like a casino for a dog with all the smells, sights and sounds to explore, so like all the other tricks, begin training this one in a calm environment indoors. Put your dog on their leash, and have your clicker, some treats in your pocket, and your training regimen ready.

The first step is to have your dog stand on either side of you with the leash on. Make the leash a bit slack, but only a foot or so. Your dog should not be able to go far. Have your dog sit. Take a treat out of your pocket and put it in front of your dog's nose. As you take a step forward, move the treat forward as well. As your dog walks forward, say the 'heel' command, and click and reward with the treat if your dog follows your step, matching your stride. Take another step, and repeat the same process. Keep doing this process, and then slowly remove the guided treat in front of the dog's nose.

Practice going for walks in different areas of your home before going on an actual walk. A real walk will be the true test for your 'heel' command! 'Heel' can be a tough one to learn, but your dog can do it with your guidance and patient teaching.

13 Kiss (Licks)

Now that you know the five essential commands, we can move on to more fun tricks for you and your dog! The first trick will be "kiss," or for your dog to lick you on the face or hand.

You'll need something that you can smear onto your hand or cheek that is dog-friendly, such as peanut butter or cream cheese. You'll also probably want to keep a damp towel or wash cloth on hand — this could get messy!

First, you'll want to take a small dab of the peanut butter or cream cheese and place it on your cheek (if you'd like to teach your dog to kiss somewhere else, like hand or lips, put the treat there instead.) Instruct the dog to sit in front of you. Once you feel they are settled and not sniffing or jumping on you to get to the treat, say the "cue phrase." This will be the word or set of words you'll use to instruct the dog to do the command in the future. Most commonly used for this is "kiss," "give kisses," or "gimme sugar," but you can come up with anything that you like. Once you've said the cue phrase, you'll want to lean into your dog so they can reach the treat. The rest is up to them!

They will most likely sniff the treat and lick it off of your face. You can practice this trick for a few minutes several times a day. After two weeks or so, (or sooner, if you think your dog has picked it up quicker), you can wean your dog off the treat and just give the command with no aid. If you notice they still need it, alternate times of using it and doing without. Soon, your dog will be giving you kisses every time you ask!

14 BARK ON COMMAND (SPEAK)

TEACHING YOUR DOG TO BARK on command has many benefits, but one of the biggest is to cure unwanted barking and growling. Many dog owners are hesitant to teach their dog to bark on command because they think it will provoke them to bark whenever they want, but this is a myth. Teaching your dog to speak only when told will actually help stop unwarranted barking every time a stranger walks by or a car pulls up, and will let them know they are only supposed to bark when you tell them to. A few other benefits to this trick would be that teaching your dog to bark on command is a useful base for teaching other more complex tricks down the line, such as learning to bark at suspicious strangers, learning to count, or controlling their growl.

Step one, get your dog to bark however you can. If you know that the dog barks at the sound of the telephone or the ringing of the doorbell, do one of those things purposefully. When they bark, say "speak," click and then give treat. Make sure you are only rewarding your dog with a click and reward when you use the verbal command or are initiating the barking. Only give reward for a single bark, teaching your dog to bark excessively will not be as effective. Do this several times a day for a few days, after that, try giving the command "speak" on its own. If they obey and bark, give them a jackpot treat — something that will show them that was a very good and smart thing to do. Once your dog becomes more accustomed to the command, try making it even more controlled. For example, once they need no aid besides the verbal command to speak, have them sit and give you all their attention. Once you feel they are completely undistracted, give them the "speak" command. This will help control the barking even more, letting the dog know they are not to speak unless they are totally focused on you and told to do so.

For dog owners with quieter dogs who don't tend to bark at anything, you'll have to start smaller. Figure out each small sound your dog makes and the cues for it. If your dog growls slightly at a certain movement, click and give treat every time they do that with the verbal command "speak." Once they've picked up on that, only click and reward when the growls become louder. Become more selective when rewarding the dog, and soon they will learn that they need to be louder to earn the reward.

15 SHAKE/HIGH FIVE

TEACHING YOUR DOG TO SHAKE is typically very simple and very entertaining for those watching. For some dogs who are a bit more stubborn, it could be more difficult, but there are ways to get even the most stubborn dog to shake hands, even if it takes a little more effort. We will go into two different ways in which you can teach your dog to shake hands or "give paw" that are guaranteed to make your dog the life of any party.

One note here — if your dog doesn't like his or her paws being touched, it might be best to avoid teaching this trick until later. You will need to desensitize your dog to having their paws touched, and you may want to look into more advanced training for this issue, depending on how sensitive they are.

First, just like with any trick, you'll want to stay patient — this trick may take a little while for your dog to pick up on, but once they do, it will be very easy to command. You'll want to get a handful of small dog treats or their favorite food that won't take too long to chew. Starting out, you'll want to get your dog to sit. Take a treat in the palm of your hand and show the dog that you're holding it. Close your fist around the treat and hold your fist close to their paw and just a bit off the ground (about an inch or so). If your dog stands up, have them sit again. If your dog lifts their paw at all, even the slightest bit, or shifts their weight from one paw to the next, tell them "yes" and give them the treat. If your dog is comfortable with the click and reward method, you can do that instead. Some dogs will bat at your hand with their paw to get the treat, so if this happens, open your hand to reveal it and tell them "yes," or whatever your chosen signal is for a good behavior.

While this is happening, your other hand should be held out flat and ready to "shake" when your dog lifts their paw. You should shake their paw with your other hand while they are eating the treat. The key to this is consistency, and rewarding your dog immediately once they've done the right thing, even if it's just slightly at first. Once they are finally lifting their paw fully off the ground and into your hand, match the action with the verbal command "shake" or "give paw." Gradually phase out the treats, and soon enough they should learn to shake with just the verbal command.

If your dog is a bit more stubborn, you'll have to take a more direct approach. Start by having your dog sit in front of you. Take their paw in your hand and lift it up to shake. While doing this, give treat and say your verbal command. Every time you perform this action, praise your dog to let them know this is a good thing they are doing, as some dogs may be fearful or worried they're being punished if their paws are being touched. Continue this daily until they respond to just the verbal command without you having to take their paw on your own. Just like with the other way, phase out the treats over time until your dog learns to react just to the verbal command. If you prefer the click and reward method, feel free to do this after grabbing the dog's paw and shaking. No matter how you prefer to teach the dog this command, make sure you aren't focusing more time on it daily than 5-10 minutes. Any more than that and both you and your dog can become frustrated. If after 10 minutes your dog seems antsy and uncooperative, end your training for the day on a good note — perform an action they do well at so they feel confident at the end and excited for the next day.

Another variation on the "shake" command is the "high five" command. This command is very similar to the other, but instead of giving you a hand shake, the dog's paw will raise as if you two were high-fiving. To begin, sit on the floor facing your dog. If they tend to get distracted easily or wander during training, keep them on a leash. Perform the same action as the first step in which you show the dog a treat and clasp your fist around it. Hold your fist a few inches away from the dog's snout, just under their face. If your dog sniffs your hand or stands, don't say anything. Instruct them to sit back down and wait until they paw at your hand, almost like a smack. Once they do, open your hand and give the treat followed by praise (if you prefer the click and reward method, do so now).

Do this multiple times until they've picked up on it. After a few times, remove the treat from your hand and keep them behind your back or in your pocket, out of view of the dog. Hold up your fist as though you have the treat and wait for them to paw your hand. After they do, reward them with a treat and praise. When they have gotten this down with no treat in the hand, raise your hand as if you were giving a high five instead. If the dog begins to paw at your hand this way, reward with a treat and praise. Once your hand is turned out this way and the dog performs properly, match it with a verbal command such as "high five." Perform this action for 5-10 minutes daily along with "shake," or wait until your dog has already learned to shake before teaching this if you feel your dog may become confused between the two.

16 Fetch

FETCH MAY SEEM LIKE ONE of the commands that is instinctive to a dog — one that you may not have to teach them. For some dogs this may be true. But if your dog doesn't understand fetch, do not worry. A lot of dogs don't pick up the idea of fetch without being taught how to do so, and it's a very simple concept for your dog to learn. If your dog isn't one to catch an object and bring it back, it's probably true that your dog is one of two other types: You throw a toy and your dog stares at you, unsure of why you would throw away a perfectly good toy, or you throw a toy and your dog chooses to play "keep away" rather than fetch. What can you do to help your dog master this simple game? There are a few easy steps.

First, if your dog is one who tends to sit and stay, not understanding the idea of running after a toy, you'll want to start out by teaching them to chase after the object. In order to jumpstart this chase, you can offer them treats and praise for chasing the object. Place the object near them and tell your dog to get the object. Once they do, reward them with a treat and praise. If your dog responds well to the click and reward method, do so after your dog has retrieved the object. Once you have given them the treat and praise, take the toy away. When they have gotten the hang of this, throw the toy a short distance and continue the process. When they run for the object, immediately reward them. Repeat this process until you can reliably get your dog to chase the object time after time. One way to encourage the chase, if your dog is struggling with that, is to throw the toy and hold your dog back by the chest for a few seconds. This will urge them to naturally tug against you and want to get the toy. While holding them back, encourage them with verbal praise such as "go get it" or "get the toy." Once you let them go, they will run for the toy and you can reward and praise them.

After your dog learns to chase the object, the next goal is getting them to actually bring it back to you. This is also good for those whose dogs like to chase the ball but not bring it back. If your dog is one of these, bringing in a second toy will help. Throw the second toy in the opposite direction, and the dog will probably drop the first toy to get to the second one. This will get them accustomed to the fact that they will have to run back to you after each chase. After they get used to this, try calling them to bring the first toy to you while showing them the second one. This will motivate them to bring you the toy in order to get the second one, and will get them used to bringing you a toy every time they catch one.

When your dog gets used to bringing a toy back, it's time to teach them to bring it right to you. If they drop the toy in front of you or a little ways from you, back away while saying "all the way" or "bring it." Once they walk to the spot where you were originally standing, praise them and offer a treat if needed, then throw the toy again. If your dog's issue is not letting go of the toy, command "drop it" and put a treat by their nose, since this will encourage most dogs to drop the toy and go for the treat. This will be taught in more detail later on under the command "leave it." The most important part of fetch is making sure you're playing with something the dog is actually interested in. It may take a few times for you to figure out which toys your dog likes best, but try different objects, such as balls, ropes, and frisbees until you find your dog's favorite. After a few times of practice, your dog should be able to perform these commands without reward, as playing fetch with their owner will be rewarding enough!

17 GO TO BED

TEACHING YOUR DOG TO "go to bed" is a very useful command to learn. It can help keep them stay calm when strangers are over or get them out of your way when needed. With "go to bed" the dog learns to go lay down in a designated crate or bed that will be seen as their safe space. The first step when teaching your dog to go to bed is to reward them when they notice their bed, since this is the first thing they'll have to do in order to be able to go there on their own. Once the dog notices the bed, you can click and reward or use praise like "yes" or "good" to indicate they are on the right track.

It's important to stay patient and keep things exciting and short for the dog. There's only so long that they can handle trying to learn something in one day, so keep training for this short but persistent. Don't get frustrated and angry when they have trouble finding their bed or following directions; punishment or anger is never the right way to train a dog. If you seem excited and happy about your dog doing the right thing, they will follow. Some dogs may get stressed during this activity, and will show it in ways such as sniffing the ground, licking private parts, or scratching a random itch. If you notice these behaviors in your dog, give them a few minutes to recuperate before trying again.

Keep in mind that moving the bed around will help in training — it helps teach the dog that it's the bed they need to be focusing on, not just one particular spot in the home. Also, every time you pick up the bed and move it, it keeps it interesting for the dog and keeps them focused. Once the dog becomes comfortable and begins to move closer to the bed, click and treat. If they finally step on the bed, instruct them to sit and lay down.

Experiment with how long you can keep the dog on the bed. After they begin to get more comfortable, start to use the verbal command of "go to bed."

As they become more and more comfortable with the command, begin to move the bed further distances from you and into different rooms. Make sure the dog is comfortable with each step before moving onto the next one. Another simple way to teach your dog to go to bed — which can also be incorporated into the first method — is to teach your dog that everything good happens on their bed. Leave treats on the bed for them to find, feed your dog on the bed, leave their favorite toys on the bed, etc. This will teach the dog that bed is a good place to be, so that when they are commanded to go there, it will seem like a good thing instead of a punishment, and they will be more inclined to listen.

18 ROLL OVER

TEACHING YOUR DOG TO ROLL over is fun for all involved once they master it. The main component to this trick is making sure your dog knows the "Down" command, which you already have completed at this point! Step one is to tell your dog "down" or "lay down." Kneel down beside your dog with a small treat (so that they are aware of it) near their head on the side of their nose. Bring your hand around their nose to their shoulder, forcing them to roll down onto their side. Try this part a few times with praise and a treat (or click and reward) each time they do it correctly. Make sure they are laying their body flat on their side with their head on the floor to ensure proper positioning for the next step.

After they've done this, continue the path of your hand with a treat from their shoulder to their backbone. This will cause their head to follow the treat, forcing their body to flip over. Once they are rolled over, continue the movement of your hand away so they flip all the way over back onto their arms. Try this a few more times. Once they can follow this consistently, add the verbal command "roll over" with the treat and praise. As you continue in your practice, gradually wean the treats away as well as lessen the hand movements. After enough practice, your dog will be able to perform the trick after just a verbal cue. Remember to always praise and reward their hard work, even once it has become easy for them. They only ever want to please you, so make sure to let them know you're happy with them!

19 PLAY DEAD (BANG BANG!)

NOW THAT YOUR DOG IS a master of rolling over, we can tackle how to play dead! Just like all the other commands we've completed so far, in order to teach your dog to play dead, you'll need a handful of their favorite treats, and if you're using a clicker, this is a great time to use it. To get your dog in position to play dead, you'll want to get them on their side like you did for rolling over. Have them lay down, and hold a treat close to their nose, pulling it around to their shoulder in order to get them flat on their side. Once they are on their side, praise them with a "yes" or "good," or click your clicker, then reward with a treat. Repeat this step several times.

Once the dog seems to complete this step with ease, add a cue word and hand signal. Most common among dog owners for this trick is the "play dead" or "bang bang!" cue, with a hand signal looking like a gun. Repeat the first step while using the hand signal and verbal command. Practice this trick several times a day for about 5-10 minutes, and after a few days your dog will be a pro! When the dog is accustomed to the trick, some owners like to have fun with it, saying things like, "Would you rather be a cat, or would you rather be dead?" in order to get the dog to play. What a great trick to impress your friends or have a good laugh with!

20 Spin

Teaching your dog to spin is not only a fun and entertaining trick to know, but it helps stretch out your dog, keeping them limber and helping prevent injuries. One thing to keep in mind while teaching your dog this trick is that speed is not important right away — some dogs spin around very quickly, others much slower, but controlling the speed of the turn is something you shouldn't worry about until the dog has mastered their skill in spinning.

The best way to get the dog to become accustomed to the act of spinning is to lure them. W the help of a treat, hold your hand right at the tip of the dog's nose, allowing them to smell the treat. Lure them around in a 360-degree spin by pulling your hand in a circular motion, motivating the dog to follow the treat. Try to only work with one direction at a time so as not to confuse your dog. Once you've completed a full circle, click and reward or praise the dog and give them the treat. Begin to pull your hand further and further above the dog's head, still using a cookie at first to lure them.

When your dog has reached a level of understanding, your hand should be about a foot above their head as you circle around them without a treat. After they've successfully begun completing the spin without the lure, add a verbal cue such as "spin." If you'd like to teach the dog differentiating directions such as "left" and "right," use those cue words. This will take a bit longer for the dog to learn, but it will give you more variety in your tricks. Begin to fade away the hand signals until the dog knows to spin when the cue is heard. Soon enough, your dog will be spinning circles around you with just the verbal cue!

21 Sit Pretty (on Hind Legs)

MANY OF US HAVE HEARD people telling their dogs to beg (or more frequently, not to beg), which is another term for "sitting pretty." This is a trick in which your dog will learn to sit on only their hind legs with their wrists bent to seem like they are begging. First, as always, you will want to get a handful of treats that your dog likes to help motivate them to perform the trick. Have your dog sit. Take a treat and allow them to see it. Hold it just above their nose and begin to raise the treat slowly. This should encourage the dog to raise their front paws off the ground to follow the treat. As soon as their front paws come off the ground, praise or click and reward with treat.

Continue to raise the treat higher, forcing the dog off their front legs even more, and praising them every time they get higher. The end goal is to get them completely off their front paws and resting fully on their hind haunches. Some dogs have a hard time finding their balance when in this position, so during the beginning of training, allow the dog to rest their front paws on your arm while they get used to the position if needed. Once the behavior is performed consistently and accurately, match the hand signal with a verbal cue such as "sit pretty" or "beg." Begin to phase out the hand signals until your dog understands to perform only with the verbal cue.

22 LEAVE IT

THERE ARE MANY INSTANCES IN which the command "leave it" will be beneficial to your dog. Some could be as simple as when we earlier learned how to teach your dog fetch, and others could be when something dangerous is dropped to the floor that could harm your dog and you don't want them to grab it and run. This command could, in fact, save your dog's life — because we all know that sometimes those little guys are just too fast for us to catch up with in order to snatch something from their mouth. You'll need a few things in order to master this command, such as a leash, yummy and "boring" treats, and your clicker or praise words.

Begin this training by sitting on the floor with your dog. Keep your boring treats in your hand and your yummy treats somewhere easily accessible to you, such as your pocket. Hold your fist with the boring treats out to the dog and wait — most likely, your dog will try anything to get to these treats, but don't let them! As soon as they stop attempting to get the treats, click and reward with one of the yummy ones. Make sure to never give them a treat from your hand you're preventing them from. Otherwise, they will not understand that these treats are off limits no matter what, which is the goal. Once you go through this a few times, your dog will barely notice your fist filled with treats. When you see this change, begin to pair it with the verbal command "leave it" before presenting the closed fist. Make sure your dog has mastered this before moving onto the next step.

Next, you want to step up the difficulty for your dog. Raise your fist, give the "leave it" command, and open your palm to expose the treats. It is likely that your dog will try to snatch them from your hand or even sniff and lick at them lightly. Do not allow them to! Before they get the opportunity to get to the treats, quickly close your first and try again. As soon as you can open your first and not get a reaction from your dog, click and reward. The goal is to reward them for leaving the treats alone. Remember to never give a treat from the training palm. After your dog has learned the "leave it" command with treats in your hand, it's time to move the treats to the floor. This all may not happen on the first time the dog is being trained, so be patient and work for 10-15 minutes on the command daily. Don't get frustrated or allow the dog to get frustrated, just be consistent and positive and your dog will learn quickly.

Now that you've moved to the next step, you will place the boring treats on the floor beneath your cupped hand. Give the "leave it" command. Once your dog has left your cupped hand alone, immediately click and reward. As they begin to get better with this, move on to the next step of un-cupping your hand from the treats and leaving them exposed on the floor along with the "leave it" verbal cue. As soon as your dog tries to steal them, quickly cup your hand over them. Do not reward until the dog leaves the exposed treats alone completely. Work on these steps regularly like the last two until your dog becomes comfortable with them, then you are ready for the last step!

For the final step, you will put your dog on the leash. Hold the leash shorter than usual but still enough that they have room to move a little. You can do this step with either treats or toys, but using both may help teach the dog that the command is not meant just for food. While holding the leash, toss the object onto the floor just out of reach for the dog. They will most likely move to get to the object. Give the verbal cue "leave it," and wait until the dog stops straining against the leash. Once they do, click and reward. Repeat this step until your dog can understand the verbal "leave it" command without being restrained.

It's important to always remember that although you should reward them once they begin to learn the command, that you should never reward them with the treat or toy you are using to keep away from them. Once they have learned to not go after the treats and toys you're training with, always reward them with something "better." This way they know that if they don't go after the good stuff, they'll have something better to look forward to. If you practice this command consistently, you will begin to see how helpful this trick can be! Not only will your dog no longer eat food dropped during dinner preparation, but they will no longer chase the neighbor's cat or pick up harmful things not intended for them.

You will probably find "leave it" helpful in many different scenarios, so it is good that you have learned this trick with your dog.

23 Yawn

Teaching your dog to yawn can be very beneficial to both you and your animal for multiple reasons. For starters, understanding why your dog yawns during certain times is important. A big reason why your dog may yawn excessively or when they are not tired is because of anxiety. A dog may yawn when they are feeling anxious or nervous, so being able to control that may help get some of their anxiety under control. Yawning is also a key way for dogs to communicate with other animals and people. Some dogs will use this as a signal that they are friendly and don't present a threat. This can be helpful to help your dog produce a yawn in social settings around other dogs or people in order to ensure their safety around your pet.

Now, it's time to get your dog to learn how to yawn on command. For starters, look out for your dog's natural tired yawns and yawns when they are anxious or stressed. This may happen when they want to go outside, they want a toy you're holding, or are nervous about getting in the car. Whenever they yawn, click and reward. It's very important that you stay alert with your clicking since teaching this behavior is all based off of your attentiveness to your dog. Clicking at just the right time will allow the dog to begin to understand why you are clicking them for a natural behavior. Once they begin to offer a yawn because they know they will be rewarded for it, begin to assign a verbal cue to it, such as "yawn," "tired," "are you tired?" etc., whatever you're most comfortable with. No matter what, consistency is key, so just make sure you're using the same phrase over and over again with the right timing.

After using the command enough for your dog to understand it, try using it without them initiating the yawn and see if it works. If you prefer to use treats over the clicking method, you'll want to withhold a treat from your dog that they are aware of. Show them the tasty treat and keep it away from them. Keep a close eye on your dog as they will most likely be confused as to what they have to do to earn the treat. Keep it out of their reach, even if they perform smart commands like sitting or laying down to earn it. At some point, your dog will yawn out of confusion or anxiousness. At this point, reward the yawn with the treat. Continue to do this and you will see that your dog will yawn sooner and sooner each time once they realize they are being rewarded for it. Finally, add your verbal command to the word and be consistent.

24 Bow

TEACHING YOUR DOG ENTERTAINING TRICKS has positive effects on both you and your dog. Dogs enjoy being rewarded with love, treats, and positive attention. People love to see their dogs doing cute things and showing it off to their friends — it's a win-win! Teaching your dog to take a bow is one of those tricks. In this trick, your dog will lean down on their elbows with their chest touching the ground and their rear end in the air. It's the perfect finishing act when you're showing off your dog's expertise at a party or gathering! All you'll need to teach this trick is dog treats and a clicker if you're using one.

First, have your dog stand facing you. Hold a treat at the tip of your dog's nose, and move it down toward the floor slowly. This will urge the dog to follow the treat, tracing their nose toward the floor. Just like with teaching your dog to spin, you will be using the luring method on this. Wait until your dog's elbows are down to the ground with their snout on the floor. Some dogs may have trouble understanding to keep their rear end in the air and will instead just lay down. If this is true for your dog, hold your free arm under their belly to hold their back end up while their chest slides to the floor following the treat. After a few times, they will catch on and won't need your arm holding up their belly to do it. Hold the pose for a few seconds before luring them back into a standing position. Click or verbally praise with "yes" or "good" and reward. Repeat this step several times until the dog does it with ease. Once it becomes easier, add the verbal cue "bow" before completing the steps. Practice this trick with your dog every day for no more than five minutes so as not to frustrate them or you.

If your dog has a harder time catching on, rewarding in smaller increments will take a bit longer but will still get the job done. If you pull the treat to the floor and your dog can only bow their head a bit toward the ground, begin by rewarding them for that. Then, don't reward them until they make closer movements toward what you're looking for. This is great for clicker training. Your dog will eventually catch on to what you're expecting of them and they will learn to follow the commands. After a few days or weeks of practice, your dog will be a professional at taking a bow!

25 Balance Item on Nose

THIS TRICK CAN BE TAUGHT to a dog while they are either seated, standing, or lying down — which you choose is personal preference. Typically, dogs are taught to be seated while learning to balance something on their nose because it is the most stable position for them. Stand in front of your dog and make sure their full attention is on you. Tell them to sit, and hold a treat in front of their face. Lower the treat right in front of their face, and place it on the top, flat part of their nose. If they begin to thrash their head around before you can balance it, gently grasp the bottom of their jaw to keep their head steady enough to hold the treat. Usually, they will flip their head to eat the treat as soon as you release their jaw, so you can hold onto it for a few seconds to let them know they're not allowed to eat the treat without your command.

Once a few seconds have passed, take the treat off their nose and reward them, letting them know that they did well. If you are using the clicker method, once you remove the treat from their nose, click and reward. Do this a few times, holding the dog's chin and removing the treat, until you leave the treat on top for them to get. Try it without holding their jaw — if they move their head to eat the treat before they're told, quickly take it away and try again. Repeat these steps until the dog learns to hold the treat on their nose without your aid. Begin to use a verbal cue, such as "okay," "get it," or "eat it." Practice this a few times every day until your dog understands to remain motionless while you place the treat on their nose, and that they are not allowed to eat it without your permission. Experiment with times — see how long you can hold the dog there before they move their face to get the treat. The ultimate goal is to get the dog to sit there for as long as possible without moving before you give them the verbal cue. Next, you can work on teaching them to flip the treat into their mouths on their own!

26 Get Leash

In order to save yourself some time and stress during a busy morning, wouldn't it be easier if your dog could get the leash themselves? It would also be easier if they could walk themselves, but let's not go too far... This next step will teach your dog how to get their own leash.

First, you'll want to introduce the word "leash" to your dog by saying it every time you put it on them. Learning names and repetition of words is the key here — once the dog understands what "leash" means and what it is, the rest is just implementing previously taught commands. Some of the basics to teach your dog this trick are the same that we learned earlier with "fetch." For starters, set the leash on the floor and encourage the dog to take it. When they do, click and reward or praise with "yes" or "good" and reward. Go toward the door and tell them to come — make sure they still have the leash. You can use verbal commands here that that already know such as "bring it" or "bring the leash." Incorporating the word leash into the training over and over again will reinforce to the dog the importance of having the leash. Once they bring the leash to you by the door, tell them to drop it. Click and reward. If they are having trouble with dropping it into your hands, do not reward them with a walk or a treat. This will let them know that when they don't hand over the leash they will not be rewarded in the end. If they bring it and drop it on the floor, repeat the steps until they drop it into your hands, then you can click and reward. Repeat these steps several times, and every time they drop the leash in your hands repeat the word "leash" for reinforcement.

Eventually, when the dog becomes more comfortable, you can eliminate the other verbal commands such as "take it, bring it, drop it," or whatever you're using to encourage them to bring you the leash. Instead, begin only using the word "leash" or "bring me the leash" to command them. Once the dog has become comfortable with this, randomly tell them to bring you the leash. If they do, click and reward them with a jackpot. Make sure you also end these training sessions with nice long walks! If the dog thinks they will get nothing out of it when bringing you the leash, they will be less inclined to follow your commands. If they know they will be rewarded with a walk, they will learn more quickly and be more eager to follow along.

27 QUIET (STOP BARKING)

THERE ARE MANY WAYS IN which you can teach your dog to stop barking, but before you can do that you have to take some preliminary steps. First, figure out why your dog is barking and remove the motivation. For example, if they always bark when people pass by outside or animals can be seen in your yard, close the curtains or put your dog in another room where they are out of sight. This will teach them that they are not allowed to have the luxury of seeing outside if they bark. If they are outside and bark at passersby or animals, bring them inside. This will have the same effect, teaching them that they aren't allowed to be outside if they bark.

If your dog barks in order to get attention, don't give them any. Ignore your dog for as long as it takes before they stop barking — don't look at them, don't touch them, don't talk to them. When they bark and receive affection or attention from you in order for them to stop, it teaches them that they just need to bark to get what they want. When you take away that reward, they don't use it as a resource anymore. Once they quiet down, reward them with a treat. If you're using the click method, click and reward after they stop barking completely. The key here is to stick it out for however long it takes for them to stop barking. If you wait an hour for them to stop and get fed up and tell them to stop, the next time they will only bark for longer. This teaches them that if they bark long enough they will eventually get attention. If your dog is crated or put in a room alone and barks for attention, turn your back or leave the room and give them no attention, not even to quiet them. As they catch on that once they're quiet they get a treat, you should lengthen the time you wait before they get rewarded. Begin by rewarding them for short periods of quietness and move up to longer amounts of time.

If you'd like to teach your dog the "quiet" command, you have to first begin by having them bark on command (I know, it sounds backwards). Luckily, we already mastered that command, and you now know how to do it. Begin in a quiet and non-distracting environment. Command your dog to speak. When they start barking, use the verbal cue "quiet" and stick a treat in front of their nose. Praise them for being quiet or click and reward. Repeat this step a few times. Once they have become accustomed to the quiet command in a calm setting, practice it in increasingly distracting situations like when someone knocks on the door or when the phone rings.

Another way to tackle barking is to pair it with an incompatible behavior. For example, if your dog barks when the doorbell rings, tell them to "go to bed" once they hear it. At this point, they are already familiar with that command, so they will understand they must follow your rule. If they're too hyped up to listen, toss a treat onto their bed and tell them to go to bed. When they're in their bed earning the treat, open the door. If they get up, close the door immediately. Repeat these steps until they learn to stay on the bed while the door opens.

Something as simple as keeping your dog tired is also important to stop them from excessive barking. Ensure they are getting sufficient physical and mental exercise every day in order to release that pent-up energy. You know how they say, "A tired dog is a good dog?" A dog who gets adequate exercise is much less likely to bark from stress, anxiety, or boredom. Giving your dog an outlet for their energy or anxieties will help your training process to be much easier.

28 Conclusion

THANK YOU FOR READING THIS book, and I hope you learned how to train your dog and how to teach 20 awesome commands. Show them off at your next party! Your dog will love to perform for others (or maybe he or she just loves all the extra treats they'll get!)

By now, you should have a good understanding of how to improve your relationship with your dog, and now you should be brought closer together through dog training.

I hope you had fun. Keep this manual handy, as some tricks take a while to teach, so you can space them out over the course of weeks, months or years. They won't happen overnight, but as you can see, the training is part of the fun.

YOUR FEEDBACK IS IMPORTANT TO ME

Dear Reader,

Thank you for taking the time to read this book. I hope you got a lot out of it and learned something you can apply to your own life.

If you have any feedback, positive or negative, I'd love to hear from you. I personally read all the reviews on my Amazon page, and hope you'll take a minute to tell me (and other readers) what you think.

Go to this book's amazon page or enter this URL in your to go straight to the review page for this book: bitly.com/dogtricksreview

Thank you!

—Shannon O'Bourne